HOW TO BECOME A SUCCESSFUL ENTREPRENEUR

A PRACTICAL GUIDE

TO TRANSITION FROM EMPLOYEE

TO SUCCESSFUL BUSINESS OWNER

By:

Boris Timm

[:Copyright:] © 2019 by Boris Timm - amazon.com/author/boris-timm

All rights reserved. No part of this publication may be reproduced, distributed, or transmitted in any form or by any means, including photocopying, recording, or other electronic or mechanical methods, without the prior written permission of the publisher, except in the case of brief quotations embodied in critical reviews and certain other noncommercial uses permitted by copyright law.

Although every precaution has been taken to verify the accuracy of the information contained herein, the author and publisher assume no responsibility for any errors or omissions. No liability is assumed for damages that may result from the use of information contained within.

Table of Contents

Welcome to the World of the Entrepreneurs! 1

Chapter 1 4

   Who is Actually an Entrepreneur?

Chapter 2 7

   Characteristics and Qualities of an Entrepreneur

      Characteristics Of Entrepreneurs

Chapter 3 17

   Defining Entrepreneur Consulting Options

Chapter 4 22

   What Does it Take to Be an Entrepreneur

Chapter 5 26

   Goal Setting in Entrepreneurship

Chapter 6 36

   Developing a Business Plan

Chapter 7 49

   How to Become a Successful Entrepreneur Today

Chapter 8 54

   How to Become a Successful Entrepreneur on the Web

Chapter 9 65

   How to Become a Successful Entrepreneur and Avoid the Mistakes of Others

Chapter 10 68
   Sourcing for Money to Start Your Business
Chapter 11 81
   Does Branding Your Business Matter?
Chapter 12 90
   Legal Aspect of Your Business
Chapter 13 101
   Marketing Your Business as an Entrepreneur
Conclusion 113
   Risks of Entrepreneurship
   Rewards of Entrepreneurship

WELCOME TO THE WORLD OF THE ENTREPRENEURS!

"You have to see failure as the beginning and the middle, but never entertain it as an end." - Jessica Herrin

I came to realize that entrepreneurship has been there for so many years and that there are many people who cannot define correctly who an entrepreneur is. This is because there is a disagreement of whether entrepreneurs are born or made.

By the way, are entrepreneurs born or made? I'm afraid if we start this discussion we might not come to a conclusion.

Why is it that there is no universal agreement whether entrepreneurs are born or made? First, entrepreneurs are born because there are some people who have come up with new business ideas that are currently recognized as successful businesses but these people were never educated on how to become entrepreneurs.

On the other hand entrepreneurs are made because there are some successful entrepreneurs who have studied entrepreneurship courses (diploma and degree programs) offered by colleges and universities.

Is it true that people have not succeeded in defining who a true entrepreneur is?

According to what I studied in high school under the subject of business, an entrepreneur is "a person who sets up successful businesses and business deals." But this definition does not bring out a clear definition because not everyone who sets up a business and is running it successful is an entrepreneur.

There is more of who a true entrepreneur is other than setting up a business and running it successfully.

Economists and business people don't seem to agree on what characterizes a true entrepreneur. From economists' point of view, "the entrepreneur is one who is willing to bear the risk of a new venture if there is a significant chance for profit".

Others emphasize the entrepreneur's role as an innovator who markets his innovation. Still other economists say that entrepreneurs develop new goods or processes that the market demands and are not currently being supplied.

The concept of entrepreneurship first came into existence in the 1700s. Since then it has evolved to what it is now today. Despite the failure of defining who a true entrepreneur is, we can all agree that entrepreneurs play a major role in enhancing the lives of people in many different ways. They come up with new ideas which have led them to create business organizations.

These organizations apart from creating job opportunities directly or indirectly they also serve people in various ways. Entrepreneurs are viewed as people who either create new products or improve the existing products so as to solve problems facing people.

If you have an inclination to be an entrepreneur, then this is the ebook that will open your vision to see all the things you need to know about entrepreneurship.

Fasten your seat belt and let us ride into the land of the entrepreneurs.

CHAPTER 1

Who is Actually an Entrepreneur?

"The entrepreneur always searches for change, responds to it, and exploits it as an opportunity - By Peter Drucker."

Entrepreneurs are those who bring ideas from the world of forms to the world of reality. Entrepreneurs are those who dream and never go back to sleep until their dreams becomes real. Entrepreneurs are those who start from little or nothing, to build something from nowhere.

Entrepreneurs are people who have an unending desire to create business, whether they have ideas or not. Entrepreneurs are those who give life to ideas and create wealth from nothing. Entrepreneurs are people who can put everything they have in order to get everything they desire. Entrepreneurs are those that can reproduce themselves and also make others reproduce themselves.

Entrepreneurs are those who can easily discover the talent in others and harness it to the maximum. Entrepreneurs are those who employ the best heads, even when they did not even see the four walls of the university. They pay professors salaries and keep a lot of graduates on their payroll.

Give an entrepreneur a mountain, he will create a tunnel. Give him a beach, he will turn it into a resort. Give him a stone, he will carve it into a monument. Give him a computer, he will build a cybercafe. Ideas, dreams and aspirations in the hands of an entrepreneur can never die without being fulfilled.

Where can we find him or are you the one? Entrepreneurs do not desire to be the best authors until their experience becomes the best book ever read. Entrepreneurs never become the best motivators until their motivation builds an industry of people. Entrepreneurship is not about power and might.

Entrepreneurship is not just about ideas if not, every dreamer would have been an entrepreneur. Entrepreneurship is not all about going to school, if not, professors would have had the largest enterprises on earth. In fact, the world's richest entrepreneurs are drop-outs.

Entrepreneurship is not just all about having millions, if not, all those who won millions in promos and lotteries would have had their names written on the pages of time as the greatest entrepreneurs that ever lived. Entrepreneurship is not about being forceful, if not, generals would have commanded the greatest industry on earth.

Are you one? If not, it is not too late to start up now!

CHAPTER 2

Characteristics and Qualities of an Entrepreneur

"Don't let others convince you that the idea is good when your gut tells you it's bad." - Kevin Rose

We can describe who a true entrepreneur is by using the trait approach. Under this approach, the common traits successful entrepreneurs possess describes if a person is a true entrepreneur. The traits are:

1) Taking Risks: They take risks after they have discovered viable business opportunities. They already know that business ideas which have got high risks are the ones which yield high profits. Generally speaking, successful entrepreneurs have taken risks to be where they're now.

2) Passion: Whatever the business idea they come up with, they have passion for it. Passion keeps successful entrepreneurs going by being focused.

3) Hardworking: Successful entrepreneurs have a common trait of working hard. They work hard in seeing that all the tasks of the business are completed on time and efficiently.

4) Optimistic: Optimism is the trait that successful entrepreneurs have in common. They believe that in the future their ideas will be successful businesses. They have no room for doubting their business ideas.

5) Good Leadership: They have the trait of good leadership. Successful entrepreneurs know how to motivate their employees so that they give their best in attaining success. They create policies and goals for their businesses. They oversee that these policies are followed and the goals are accomplished on time.

6) Determined and Persistent: Successful entrepreneurs are determined and persistent in making their new business ideas successful. They don't give up after experiencing some failures in executing some tasks but they're persistent and determined because they're motivated by success and not money. For them, money is only a reward they get.

7) Flexible: Entrepreneurs who have succeeded respond to market needs swiftly. Whenever there are changes in market needs they respond to them swiftly so as not to lose their customers.

They search for opportunities to exploit when a change occurs. Successful entrepreneurs have a common trait of adjusting their entrepreneurship ventures to fluctuating economic conditions.

8) Creativity: They research and come up with creative new business ideas. Successful entrepreneurs continuously innovate new ways of satisfying customers.

9) Organization Ability: Successful entrepreneurs are well organized. They organize factors of production such as labor, land and capital in running their entrepreneurship ventures.

With all the above information, I urge you not to fail to appreciate what a true entrepreneur is still working on. This is because a true entrepreneur never gives up no matter the failures he experiences in executing some tasks. He is optimistic that one day his business idea will be a successful business.

Strong entrepreneurship spirit is unshakable and defies logic.

While you will discover a number of qualities that make up an entrepreneur, there are a few that are so exclusive that you actually can't be one without them. The one that tends to become the most important is the ability to stay focused on the prize, or the end game.

This plays into a lot of other facets of what an entrepreneur is, that without it nothing else seems to make sense.

By having the ability to keep that degree of laser like focus an entrepreneur can look past the challenges that face them each day and remember why they got started in the business in the first place. Without that they'd be like a lot of other business owners who are ready to throw in the towel when things get tough.

So to clarify one thing. A small business owner and an entrepreneur are not automatically the same thing. There are lots of business owners who are not entrepreneurs.

They got into business because they couldn't find a job, or they saw it as an alternative investment to something else like stocks or real estate. An entrepreneur, however is in business to win, plain and simple.

They need the brass ring and the pot of gold at the end of the rainbow. As opposed to the person who needs to make a living, who would bolt in a minute if a good job came along.

Entrepreneurs Value Education

Another impact that the "unwavering focus on a goal" has on entrepreneurs, is their eagerness to master whatever they have to. Among the understated entrepreneur qualities is the commitment to learning.

People see entrepreneurs as gunslingers, riding off in to the west taking wild chances and fighting in the street or wherever they need to so that they can win the day.

The truth is that entrepreneurs are very calculated in most of their moves. They have invested the effort and time to learn and understand the needs of their market.

They've also worked hard to gain the required business knowledge and acumen to drive a business. Last but not least, they generally possess a very keen understanding of the competition and know very well what it'll take to beat them in their common market.

To this end, entrepreneurs will even bring in expertise where they don't have it. Their pride is in reaching their goal and if they need help and expertise to get them their, they're going to take it.

Not Sweating The Little Things - One Of The Best Entrepreneur Qualities

Because they're educated on business, the market and their competition, entrepreneurs have a greater ability to understand how to achieve their goal. They also know they can and will attain their goal.

This is why they don't let the every day distractions get in their way. One of the biggest challenges with any business is that it never goes as intended. That is true for all business's. The fact is that there are always surprises, no matter how organized you are.

The ability to roll with these issues is greatly impacted by their capacity to remain focused on the big picture. Get lost in the late delivery, or the employee that quit, or the computer crash and you'll rapidly be out of business.

Don't get me wrong, entrepreneurs get frustrated too, but they do not let it hold them back. That's why I feel that this capacity to keep focused on the big picture is really among the most important entrepreneur qualities.

Characteristics Of Entrepreneurs

One of the key characteristics of entrepreneurs is their ability to keep focused. If you're a family member or friend, that can seem like a detriment. But if you are depending on their success in business, it is actually an asset.

To be more specific an entrepreneur is focused on the prize, or the pot of gold at the end of the rainbow. There are many who would focus on the negative elements of any situation they're in. But entrepreneurs shift past the negatives, discover solutions and then keep their eyes steadfast on the top of the mountain.

The counter for that personality, is the one who gets lost inside the daily muck of attempting to make a business succeed. They are the ones that dread their business all the time, since they are fearful of what is going to hit them next. This is one the key separating issues between those who are and those who are not, entrepreneurs.

The second characteristic that works in harmony with the first one is the ability to be solution oriented. A true entrepreneur will perceive problems as a challenge or an opportunity. What they recognize is that these challenges exist in every business. Which implies that every business owner has to face issues and the vast majority of them fold under the pressure? Because of this, that entrepreneur is aware that much of their competition will vanish over time since they will give up when the going gets to tough.

Entrepreneurs Prefer To Work With Mentors

This characteristic might surprise you a little bit, since most individuals perceive entrepreneurs as rugged individualists. That assessment in many respects is correct. But with regards to getting well educated in a field or project, entrepreneurs jump to the front of the line.

The strongest entrepreneurs have a powerful enthusiasm for books, seminars, meetings and presentations that can help them better comprehend how to succeed in their business's.

Don't get me wrong, once an entrepreneur has a clear grasp of what they are trying to accomplish, they take the reins and there's no stopping them. But regularly while in the quite hours of the night, a real entrepreneur is still sitting up by the light taking in new information and looking at ways to make their business a bit more successful.

Entrepreneurs don't just learn from materials, they also learn from others. It is not uncommon to find a true business leader involved with round table groups or consultants to help them get to their next level in their business.

This ties into the idea of staying focused on the prize. If a leader is lacking in the ability to get to a higher level, they will find that information where ever they need to look for it.

Entrepreneurs Respect And Value Their Time

Time is valuable for an entrepreneur. There are 24 hours in per day, what you do with them will decide your success.

When you have a clear sense of the goal, you will be able to weigh your judgements against that goal.

In other words, you have 8 hours to complete a project, your friend wants to know if you want to play golf. If you are focused on your organization and you value those eight hours, you will pass on the golf game.

There are many more characteristics of an entrepreneur. But if you keep in mind that; focus on the goal, an unwavering promise to never give up plus the premium put on the value of time, are the cornerstones. Then you'll have completed a key first step towards business success.

CHAPTER 3

Defining Entrepreneur Consulting Options

"One of the greatest skills of leadership is being unflappable. Anytime you do anything in the world; there's going to be criticism." - *Arianna Huffington*

Before you inquire about consulting services, you need to ask yourself if you are actually an entrepreneur, or just someone trying to survive in a business. While the two may well seem to be the same thing, they are very different.

With the current economy, there are many people who find themselves starting business's who are not entrepreneurs. There are some who have checked out how the companies they work for have been run and just felt that they had a better idea.

Or they were convinced they could run a business better. While an individual in this situation might be an entrepreneur, the situations themselves don't make you one.

Entrepreneurs are a different breed, they're willing to try and do anything and everything it takes to succeed in their business's. They do not know what the word "no" looks like, they study their markets as well as their competition and they're extremely solution oriented.

If you are a person who would like to start a company, but is just prepared to risk a small amount of funds, you may want to remain at your current job, or find one.

If you are a person who has tried different things, but given up following adversity, you may not be ready to be an entrepreneur.

Regardless of whether you're thinking that this time it's going to be different, you actually need to try and do some soul searching before you make the decision to leap. You may think I'm attempting to turn you off to becoming an entrepreneur and you would be correct.

Unless you are actually ready for that battle, don't jump in, there is a lot of risk here. Remember nearly all business's fail in the first few years. If you don't like the odds, you have to really re-assess where you are.

How To Make Consulting Simple

If you are still reading and haven't decided that I am a pain in the rear, then you may really have what it takes to become an entrepreneur. Keep in mind, just because you are in business, does not imply you are one.

So let's take this to the next step. I can't answer all your questions with this short article, but what I can do would be to start to steer you in the right direction. There are three types of consulting situations:

1) You are anticipating starting a company and need help with the decision, or how to get started.

2) You are in business and want to work out how to grow your business to the next level, or maybe just get it growing period.

3) You're in deep trouble with your small business and you are desperate for information on how to save it.

I will speak to each of these different types of situations in my next three blog posts. But recognize, that in every one of these steps you still have to ask yourself, "Am I An Entrepreneur"?

Deciding If You Really Need A Consultant?

There are lots of ways to find the answers to your questions. I was once advised by one of my mentors to find someone who actually knew what they were doing and do the same thing.

I firmly believe in that philosophy. So, I will pass on to you, that you can find the right person in the form of a consultant, or you can also find tools and methods that can help you get there without a direct relationship.

There are trade offs with both options. A consultant will charge you a lot more money, but will tend to get pretty deep into your company. If they're good, then you will get a return on your money.

Using tools will teach you how to resolve the issues yourself and will typically cost you a lot less up front. However the downside of tools and training are that they do not have a personal relationship with you and can't deal with the unique variables which are faced on a regular basis.

What I find to be the best type of entrepreneur consulting relationship is a hybrid of both. I will clarify this in more detail in the final part of this series.

CHAPTER 4

What Does It Take To Be An Entrepreneur

"When you are building a startup, it's difficult. You have to give 100%, and you have to be committed. Solving the problem has to be personal or else you're going to disintegrate." - Sean Rad

It is my considered opinion that entrepreneurs are in fact a rather small percentage of people who share a number of characteristics in common.

That does not mean all entrepreneurs behave in the same way, because each of those endowed with an entrepreneurial spirit will display those traits in different ways. Here is a list of those common characteristics which are characteristics entrepreneurs display.

- Optimism - Entrepreneurs consider things from a positive mindset. Problems are reinterpreted as challenges, challenges as opportunities, and opportunities as a way to move upward.

- Creativity - Entrepreneurs love the challenge of "it can't be done". For an entrepreneur, if something can't be done it simply means the thinking put into the project is not broad enough and people need to start thinking outside their particular paradigm.

- Strength - Through a combination of physical resilience, mental toughness, social awareness or emotional intelligence, entrepreneurs have an inner strength that comes to the fore when things get tough.

- Charismatic - Entrepreneurs naturally attracts good people to themselves. When entrepreneurs speak, people listen, not because they have to, but because they want to.

- Risk-taker - Entrepreneurs will launch out into the unknown without fear, will dare to go where no one has previously gone reliant on nothing more than their own resourcefulness.

- Determination - Prepared to do whatever it takes to see the task completed and the goal won, entrepreneurs will not allow themselves to be distracted or turned aside from that on which they maintain their focus.

- Free from convention - Entrepreneurs are free from the restrictive notion that the past will necessarily determine the future. Rather they see that the future is yet to be created and how it does rests entirely in their hands.

So, to be a successful business person does not automatically make you an entrepreneur. On the other hand being an entrepreneur does not automatically make you a successful business person.

There are many people down through history who could truly be called entrepreneurs, yet never made the millions of a Donald Trump or a Bill Gates. They have chosen to express their entrepreneurial spirit in other ways. Struggling for an example? How about Gandhi, Martin Luther, King, or Nelson Mandela.

Unfortunately, the concept of entrepreneurial spirit has been weakened terribly by its misuse and abuse, particularly on the Internet. But then the same thing has happened with words like 'Guru' and 'expert'.

All I ask is a little respect and consideration for those who are true entrepreneurs, Gurus and experts and let the rest of us be content with being ordinary. After all that, in itself, is quite a profound group to belong to; membership of which has not yet been fully realized by most of us.

CHAPTER 5

Goal Setting in Entrepreneurship

"Ignore the hype of the startups that you see in the press. Mostly, it's a pack of lies. Half of these startups will be dead in a year. So, focus on building your business so you can be the one left standing." - Jules Pieri.

The distance of a journey is determined by how well one is ready for the journey. For instance, when an athlete runs a triathlon, his goal is to beat his opponents and win. When a person engages in an intense workout, there is a weight goal that he or she would like to meet. When you apply for a job, your goal is to pass the interview and get accepted.

As you may notice, it is important to set a goal for yourself so that you can meet a particular objective. Without goals, your actions will all be for nothing. This is the reason why goal setting is important.

When dealing with your career, your finances or even your personal life, setting goals for yourself will allow you to create an action plan so that you can work towards, and eventually meet those goals.

Imagine that you live your life without purposes. How will you live your life? You will be ordinary, thus, you will live a mediocre life. If you don't have a goal today, you're just like a lost sheep and you are dangling in nowhere. You wake up everyday without purposes or reasons.

You live your life meaningless and you will waste your life. However, with a clear and specific goal, it will serve as a clear destination for where you are heading, giving your purpose to live on.

Goal setting will help you to stay focused in getting what you want in your life. Many people know what they want to achieve but they just don't do something to make their dreams come true. However, with a clear goal in your mind, you will remind yourself of what you want to achieve in your life and hence, it will direct you in the right direction.

This is why successful people are able to achieve what they want lightning fast, because they are focused.

It will help you to overcome procrastination. By writing down what you want to achieve, you are actually putting commitment into making it comes true. The real key in doing this is to keep reminding yourself about what you want in your life.

You want to sink the idea of achieving your goals into your subconscious mind so that you will motivate yourself into taking massive amount of action all the time.

As a whole, goal setting will allow you to turn your future plans into a reality. Here are the numerous advantages that you can get to enjoy with the help of goal setting:

Setting long-term goals for yourself will give you that drive to work harder in meeting your career or your personal objectives.

Setting short-term goals can be a great motivator, especially if you monitor your progress and celebrate your successes in each small accomplishment that you have.

Goal setting will allow you to determine the possible distractions that you may deal with in the process of meeting your long-term goals. Once these distractions are identified, you can exert an extra effort so that you will not be lured away from your goals.

Goal setting is the key to effective time management.

Goal setting will boost your self-esteem since it improves the quality of your life by letting you know exactly where you are headed in the future.

Now that you know all about the importance of goal setting, how can you begin setting such goals for yourself? Here are some useful goal setting tips that you can follow:

Start by creating a list of your short-term goals while still keeping your lifetime goals in mind.

As you slowly progress and each of your short-term goals are being met, you can move on to a broader picture: by setting your long-term goals.

Your long-term goals should span your personal, professional, financial, physical, educational, and even your public service goals. Answer these questions: - How would you like to see yourself a few years from now?

How would you like to make a difference in the lives of others? - What long-term financial goals would you like to meet? - What are your travel plans in the near future?

Remember that whether you are setting long-term or short-term goals for yourself, they should still be realistic. Knowing what you want out of life is the best way to set realistic goals for yourself.

To sum it all up, goal setting is all a matter of deciding what is important for you to achieve in this lifetime. Removing distractions, motivating yourself and boosting your confidence are the steps that you need to follow in order to meet the goals that you have set for yourself.

Committing yourself to achieving your goals is what will make your journey in life more fun, enriching and meaningful.

It could be suggested that the importance of having very clear goals is one of the things that contributes towards a person achieving success in their pursuits. The act of setting goals needs careful well thought out ideas. A goal needs to be very specific, and clear and should have very clear outcomes.

For example your goal could be to earn $60 within the next 30 days by selling books about success valued at $5 each. This could mean that you would need to earn about $2 each day for the next 30 days. To do this you could sell one book each day for 12 days and you would have achieved your goal of earning $60 within 30 days.

So you can see by having very clear goals you can achieve the things you want in life. The other point is it is important it have very clear outcomes. You have to be able to measure clearly that you have succeeded in your goals.

As you have seen from that last example, it is important to know what you want to achieve, it is useful to break it down into smaller pieces. For example the target was broken down as selling 1 book for $5 each day.

This means that once a person has sold 12 books then the target has been reached. It is also important to record effectively how many books are sold each day. In the same way it a person wanted to be a millionaire in a year, they would need to generate $19,230 each week. By knowing clearly what you want and your outcomes you can clearly see when you have achieved them.

So you should see from this that to get good results, and to achieve your goal, it is important to have very clear goals, and very clear plans how you will achieve your goals. So take time and carefully think about your goals and also think carefully about effective plans to achieve them.

You can ensure the attraction of wealth into your life through your thoughts, words, and actions. Focusing on the positive aspects of your life rather than the negative will greatly increase the speed with which wealth comes to you.

For example, if you are thinking that you will never be able to get out of debt, you are going to attract the exact thing to you. You should instead focus on the fact that you have the ability to get out of debt and you will be able to do it easily and effortlessly.

The effectivity of goal setting relies on the positivity of your goals. Goals like "I will find a better career," or "I'm going to earn twice as much as I now earn," are positive goals which you must focus on for it to become your reality. Avoid negative goals for they are just going to build up negative energy and in turn attract more negative energy in your life.

Goal setting is reliable because when you make positive statements, you will be able to achieve your goals faster. Positive statements put out positive energy to the universe as long as you believe them to be true. There must be no doubt in your mind that your goal is quite possible for you to reach.

The first step in attracting what you want is always to define and decide what you want. You must focus on the level of wealth that you would want to attract in your life for this whole thing to work. You can either be general or specific.

Either way, the feeling of excitement that you get when you set your goal to attract wealth is the most important because, this feeling is a vibrational frequency which you send out to the universe. The universe will then compensate it with the same level of frequency, bringing you the physical manifestation of your desires.

Goal setting will make you completely aware about what you really want and once you are aware of it, you can start focusing on positive energy for your desire to come to you real fast.

Focus on it with great tenacity, and soon, your desire will become a part of reality. You also have to be patient because if waiting makes you frustrated, doubt will start to build up and you are never going to reach your goal.

Start setting your goals towards attracting the level of wealth you would want to have in your life. Goal setting is as easy and as important as defining and deciding what you really want.

Goals should be specific - As far as possible try to drill down to the very specific outcome and not let your goals be vague. If you goal is to buy a big car, then just saying car is not enough. Do you want to get a Mercedes Benz or a BMW? If it is a BMW, then do you want a 3-series, 5 series, 7 series or another model? Hope you get the drift. Your goals need to be very specific.

Goals must have a deadline - A goal with no deadline is just a pipe dream. Unless you have a deadline set, you will not know how to pace yourself to achieve that goal. In addition to that there may not be a seriousness attached to your efforts since there is no pressing time line to achieve the goal. This is the reasons why deadlines are so important.

Goals must be in writing - There is just something so serious and committed about a written goal that just can't be compared to the goals that are just floating in your mind. When you put your goals down on paper, they tend to take life of their own. The very fact that you've written it down gives you clarity on what you need to achieve. Your vague thoughts are now crystal clear on paper.

These are a few ideas to make your goal setting process more robust and give you that edge that winners and achievers have over dreamers.

It is absolutely essential to dream, but to turn your dreams into reality, you must quantify them into written goals with specific timelines. That's when you've laid the foundation which if accompanied by focused action, will soon transform into a beautiful manifestation of your dreams.

CHAPTER 6

Developing a Business Plan

"Don't get distracted. Never tell yourself that you need to be the biggest brand in the whole world. Start by working on what you need at the present moment and then what you need to do tomorrow. So, set yourself manageable targets." - Jas Bagniewski.

It is common for newbies to become overwhelmed with all the information available online about internet marketing or more specifically niche marketing. That is a huge obstacle many people - new and old - will face.

This can be a good and a bad thing simultaneously. It's good because there is a ton of information available to you and it can really help your self-education.

It's bad because often the information you find may be dated or not really helpful for your situation. Niche marketing is a great opportunity for anyone who is wondering where to get started in e marketing.

There are a few things you should be aware of though before you dive in. First of all, you need to treat this as a real business if you want to achieve success. That includes writing up your own business plan.

Whether you are starting up a new business or you already have an established company, the importance of a business plan may be over looked. Yes, they can take some time to draw up but just think of your business plan as a map of a country.

Without the details and information on this map, trying to navigate yourself around a country will usually end up leaving you lost. Probably travelling the same routes over and over again, taking you 2-3 times longer to find your way.

A detailed business plan could mean your success in business. Consider this. How can you take your company in the right direction, developing the methods you need to succeed if you do not know what you are trying to accomplish. It would be like building a house with no plans and trying to put the roof on first.

Yes, you may be successful in building the roof but your house will be missing some essential pieces. You may not miss these pieces at first, but down the line you are going to be wishing you built those walls too!

A business plan plots a course for your business to follow. It allows you to determine and realize your growth but more importantly what steps are needed to be token to achieve this. It helps you figure out the materials you need in place so that you can first build a strong infrastructure for your business.

Another great thing about a business plan is that like any map it can be changed over time to represent the lay of the land. Which allows you to make any changes that need to be made to your route and to help you navigate them better.

While you are developing your business plan you will see that it will start to show you what you will need to do to be successful. Including such things as materials needed, your timeline and projected numbers for your business.

It also will show your projected income and losses, as well as how your business will do in the first months and year(s) of operations. This information is priceless.

Another important factor of a business plan is that it will show you how you need to grow. You may wonder why this is so important? Simple. It falls right under you developing a marketing plan and picking out areas/markets for you to advertise in to grow your business.

Without knowing where your business is going, there will be no way for you to develop an accurate marketing plan. These two things go hand and hand with each other.

Planning means a lot to business owners because every business involves a certain amount of risk. Most business owners achieve profit due to the calculated amount of risk that they take. This risk factor always seems to depend upon the future market conditions.

Hence if you do not plan for the future, you can never become a successful businessman. Developing a business plan is a complicated process. Here is a brief note on how to start with your plans.

Start out by writing a brief summary of your business. This should include the history of your business and other details as to how you are pertaining to outwit your competitors in the market. Hence you should make this section a bit catchy so that the reader is stimulated to read on.

Subsequently, you should describe your products and services. The benefits that your products have over other similar products out there in the market should be expressed briefly.

Next, you have to provide statistics as to how your product is expected to perform in the market.

The next part should contain information as to how you are going to promote your business. Right now, there are many different ways of promoting businesses. You can advertise your business through mass media or you can even start a website.

Next, you should describe your business processes. Outline the effectiveness of each and every process in achieving quality.

Finally, describe about the management team. The success of a business greatly depends upon its leaders. Finish the business plan by stating the skills of your management team.

Developing a business plan seems to be simple at first sight. But you will need lot more than just the procedure. It requires lots of skills to be a planner.

It is essential in today's market that a business of any size develops a business plan. In the business plan you should be ready to spell out the location for your business, plans to promote your business, and any licensing fees and other costs that will cause your investment into this business to increase substantially.

A business plan is essential, beneficial and drawing it up has no monetary costs. You will only need to invest your time to perform some research and time to write your business plan. The Internet is a great resource tool and you can find market information, statistics on growth, and other trends that you should know about your business.

The U.S. Small Business Administration states that the business plan should include such things as goals, a description of the goods and/or services that you will provide, a management plan and organizational chart, marketing plans, information about the goods and/or services, and if you will be seeking funding assistance, then you must provide financial information as well.

You can go to their website and take advantage of tools and courses that are offered to business professionals for free.

When developing your business plan you must also include how you are planning to start the business. Videos, web chats and podcasts are available that tell about best practices from other successful entrepreneurs.

If you do not have a lot of money to invest, you may look at opening a franchise. There will usually be low overhead and a smaller cost for start-up when you opt for a franchise. Another type of business entity is known as a limited liability company (LLC) and it will help provide limited liability protection and will list the members of the business, or business owners.

You will have to file documents with the secretary of state for this type business. You will have to decide on the name of your business and it cannot be the same as another company operating within your state.

Go to the state's official website and check for the availability of the name you have selected. You will have to include LLC in the legal documents along with the name you have selected.

Find the online articles of incorporation and fill in the blanks. You can also pick up or have a paper copy mailed to you if you do not have internet access.

When you prepare the articles of incorporation you will have to state the purpose for organizing the business and provide the name and address of each member. This is taken from the business plan as well. One person will have to be designated as the registered agent for the LLC.

Each member will have to sign the document and there will be a filing fee when you file with the secretary of state.

You will have to register your business with the U.S. Internal Revenue Service (IRS) and make application for the employer identification number.

You will have to provide the IRS with the date of the formation of the LLC, the type business activity, and the authorized manager. This is a free service and you can register online or call the toll free number listed on their website.

Having said all these about developing a business plan, let us take a particular look at developing a business plan for web hosting as an example.

Goals: Define your goals properly and strategy to achieve them.

Problem & Solutions: What you are going to do in any sort of crisis? How you can handle it?

Financial Issues: How much finance you have? And how long you can survive with it? How are you going to manage you business profit and loss?

Business Plan Duration: While writing a business plan you should keep that in mind, how long your business plan can survive? For that you have to do market research about the business you are going to start, it pros and cons. The success of your business can tell you how long your strategy will work?

Flexibility: Your business plan must be flexible, if things doesn't workout according to the plan than what will be your next step? Most of the people got stuck in the situation where they don't have enough flexibility in there business plan. So your business plan must be flexible enough so that you can make changes according to the twist and turn in the market.

Web hosting Business Plan: If you are planning to start a web hosting business first you have to define your business plan. Your business plan must have consists of following elements:

Define your Business Strategy: Most people got confuse in the beginning that where to start off. If you are starting a web hosting business and you don't have much idea about it started off with a small investment. Initially get a reseller web hosting plan. In reseller hosting plan you are allow to host websites as a third party.

Certain amount of space is reserved on a server for reseller account and he has permission to rent it further on the behalf of his own company. A reseller can have a shared server or he can rent a dedicated server.

Many known web hosting companies had started off as a reseller and now they are giants. So starting of as a reseller can turn out to be a huge company.

Market Analysis: Before doing anything one should analyze the conditions or situations. So as in the business you have to analyze your market place and how things work in web hosting business.

While performing a market analysis you have to keep these things in mind, what are you offering?

Where you have to start? Why you choose this business? And how you will compete? Market analysis will clarify your targeted clients and competitor so you can define your web hosting plans keeping market trends in mind.

What are you going to Offer? First you have to decide what sort of web hosting plans you can offer? There are many cheap web hosting companies offering cheap web hosting plans.

What is your uniqueness? A Reseller can provide any type of hosting plan depending on what sort of account he is using himself?

As a reseller host you can offer shared web hosting, Virtual Private Server (VPS) hosting plan and dedicated server hosting plan. Also you can define your own price and packages.

To beat your competitors you can define many discount packages. Attract them with cheap offers or provide some additional services.

Marketing Strategy: Marketing is another important aspect of a business especially when you are new. Let the others know you are here. You have to promote your web hosting business, for that you can use ads, social media, affiliate marketing and other online resources.

Marketing strategy must be defined clearly keep in mind your targeted clients and other related companies. A healthy marketing can boost up your business so your marketing campaign must offer attractive web hosting plans.

Financial Plan: Most important aspect of any business is "finance." What you going to invest in the business? How much financial resources you have? And how long you can survive with any output from your business?

Market survey will help you to decide how much investment is reQuired to set up web hosting business? Keeping in mind all the available financial resource you can define your business scale, whether you are going to start your business at small or large scale.

As if you are starting as a reseller host you don't reQuire much investment. In financial plan you have to keep record if incoming and outgoing cash so you can keep an eye on what you are earning? And how you have to spend it? Keeping in mind all these factors you can develop an efficient financial plan.

Operations and Management: As in the beginning you are starting as a reseller host so you don't have to worry about many operations. You hosting company will take care of your hardware maintenance and other complicated issues.

Also they will provide you 24/7 customer support. In future when you move on to the bigger level, you will require more space and manpower to perform these operations.

Depending on the growth of your business you have to define your needs in term of hardware, software and resources to maintain all this setup.

List down all the operations you have to perform and how many people are required to perform these operations. In web hosting business you have to maintain your many different client accounts including there web hosting plan and services they are getting.

CHAPTER 7

How to Become a Successful Entrepreneur Today

"In the age of transparency, honesty, and generosity, even in the form of an apology, generate goodwill." - Alexander Asseily.

To become a successful entrepreneur takes failure. You have to be willing to accept it and learn to make yourself better. Through experience and knowledge you will find making a certain business entity successful, as opposed to failing, is much easier to create.

When you are an entrepreneur, you are constantly learning. You are constantly looking up new things on how to add to your business. It is important that you are logical on who feeds you information, because you can find yourself in traps that are hard to get out of.

Let me give you an example as it has happened to many people who are trying to become an entrepreneur. The internet world is often times misunderstood. This leaves a gray area for sales representatives from other companies to take advantage of you.

The most important thing that any business needs is leads. People to talk to and potentially buy their product. These sales reps operating in this gray area are very aware of this concept and modify their pitch to reflect how successful you will be.

This shifts the attention from the work that is actually being done to what could possibly be obtained. So to get to the example, it is not uncommon for someone to be paying $1,000 a month for search engine optimization to be done.

However, some companies can put your company in severe risk if they are not following guidelines that are implemented and banned from sources like Google. There are many businesses out there who have shelled out tons of cash only to find their site banned a couple of months down the road.

So the first thing to do when you are looking to be a successful entrepreneur is to become aware of what works and what does not. There are trustworthy sites that you can go to get your information. When you are looking for information, look for sites that have a.gov attached to them or a reference to the actual business you are addressing like Google.

SBA.gov is a great source. Google Webmaster Guidelines is another place to gain the most useful information for if you are looking to create results with Google.

The list can go on and on, but look at the difference in who is feeding you information as opposed to a company who is just trying to sell you their product. This will most definitely save you time, energy, aggravation, and money in the long run.

Read up on some material and pretend that you know what you are talking about. If you know more than the sales rep, then it is probably not the best solution for your business. If they can take a concept and explain it more in depth, then they are most likely a better company to work with.

The companies who create results will take the time to educate their employees. The companies who are interested in only your money do not really care what the sales rep says to get the deal.

So the number one thing is to be aware that these things exist and to be precautionary moving forward with them. Even if you have everything else running perfectly, these mistakes can put you out of business.

Another important factor to mention is, "If it's not broke, don't fix it." When you are first starting a business, you often times have ideas on what will work. The only problem is that you have no data to backup your statements. There is a time to try and a time to copy.

Most successful entrepreneurs will start to work off of a strategy that they know creates results and then build off of that after they have money coming in. Most of the time, there is another business out there just like yours. They offer very similar products and have the same market to compete in. Take the time to look into their strategies. Find out what is working and what is not. This will be the shortest way to actually get the business rolling.

No matter what business model you decide to take on, the most important thing for any entrepreneur is to remain active. This is your lifeline and no one else's. You cannot sit back and rely on someone to do everything for you.

You need to engage yourself in the business every single day until it is operating how you need it to. At that point, you will have the opportunity to sit back and enjoy. It's important that you are honest with yourself and what you are willing to do to achieve your success.

Otherwise, you will try to cast blame unto others and be left with a failing business.

There are other articles out there that can help guide you on if becoming an entrepreneur is the right decision for you. Once again, be completely honest when you are answering the questions.

Some people think they want to be an entrepreneur, but don't have the drive or the capability of actually doing it. This leaves them in a worse position than sticking to their normal routine of 9-5 with a company.

There are certainly other factors to consider when looking to become an entrepreneur, such as legal business filing and merchant accounts, but these sources and mindset will help lead you in the right direction.

We are certainly here to help guide you through the process as well. Please feel free to click on the link below and we are more than happy to work with you in creating your dreams.

CHAPTER 8

How to Become a Successful Entrepreneur on the Web

"Only the paranoid survive." - Andy Grove

Becoming a successful entrepreneur in the online world is no different than becoming a successful entrepreneur in the brick-and-mortar world. Both tasks require vision, determination, and hard work.

The online world of the web offers many exciting opportunities for entrepreneurship because it is fresh, new, and exciting. The cutting edge of development has always been the most fertile ground for growing a new enterprise.

In the 1800's, the new frontier was the American west and many fortunes were made there. In the 2000's, the new frontier is the web, where many fortunes have yet to be made.

Jeff Bezos of Amazon.com is worth 162 billion dollars. Pierre Omidyar of eBay is worth just over 13 billion dollars.

David Filo and Jerry Yang of Yahoo are both billionaires. These men made fortunes on the web, and so can you.

The path to becoming a successful online entrepreneur has changed in the last few years. The over-optimism which characterized the late '90s and ultimately led to the subsequent crash in the technology sector has matured into a cautious and reasonable optimism grounded in traditional business values.

The party is over; it's time to get to work.

What Are You Going to Sell?

The #1 thing you need to succeed in business is the customer. Whether you have one customer, fifty customers, or millions of customers, it is critical to remember that customers are the foundation of any business. Without customers, you don't have a business; you have a hobby.

Going into an online business, people usually either know what they want to sell or know how they want to sell it. If the online business is an extension of a brick-and-mortar business, the entrepreneur knows what he or she has to sell and is looking for a new channel for their good and services.

If the entrepreneur is looking to start a new business online, they may not yet know what product or service will offer the best opportunities for success.

Product or Service

Every business sells either products or services, a few businesses sell both. Products are easier to sell online because they can be more easily commoditized. People have become comfortable buying known commodities online. Services which are sold online are sometimes delivered online and sometimes delivered offline.

Selling Services Online

If you choose to sell services, the next decision to consider is how the services you sell will be provided. You can choose to:

Sell your own services

Sell the services of others

Sell an automated service

Selling Your Own Services

Each of us has specific talents, abilities, and skills which can be useful to other people. These things which we have can be offered to others over the web. Perhaps you are a lawyer, a web designer, or a painter.

It should be the easiest thing in the world to create a web page to tell the world about who you are and what you can do for them.

The key to success in selling your own services over the web is to focus on the needs of your customer. For every sentence you write about yourself online, write an entire page about what you can do for your customers.

Selling the Services of Others

Selling the services of others allows us to leverage a larger workforce, and ultimately to build revenue more quickly.

Perhaps you run a lawn-care business where you sell monthly lawn-care packages to home-owners. Your lawn-care staff may be employees, or they may be independent subcontractors who do business with you at pre-negotiated rates.

In fact, you may not be in the lawn-care business at all, you may simply be in the business of being paid for generating referrals to existing lawn care firms.

Selling Automated Online Services

Selling automated online services presents a very lucrative business proposition, because it represents a potential revenue stream with very low maintenance costs. The trade-off is often in the form of considerable up-front development cost.

If you have the right idea, and the determination to follow it through to a successful conclusion, there can be no better business opportunity than selling an automated online service.

The first step, of course, is to determine what people want and what people are willing to pay for. Will people pay $9.95 for an online personality test? Will they pay $19.95 for an online personal wardrobe analysis? What would someone pay for a personalized online horoscope? How about an automated resume writing tool?

Selling Products Online

If you choose to sell products, you are not limited to selling products which you manufacture. If you are already in the manufacturing business, that is a significant advantage and the web is an excellent sales outlet for many products.

Greater opportunities exist for the rest of us by working with the distribution channel. We may buy products from manufacturers and sell then over the web, or we may buy products from wholesale distributors and sell them over the web.

We may inventory our products and oversee their shipment to customers, or we may send a request to have the products drop-shipped from our suppliers to our customers. We may never even see the products we sell.

Setting up IT

Information technology is daunting to many entrepreneurs. Each little sub-field of IT has its own culture and terminology. It is difficult for the novice to understand all of the jargon and to determine truth from hype.

You will not be successful if you try to separate yourself completely from the technology, but you will also not be successful if you immerse yourself in it. You must understand IT decisions from a business level in the same way they you understand decisions which your business makes in terms of setting prices or acquiring real estate.

The most obvious need for your new online business will be a company web site. This will introduce you to the professionals known as web designers. If your business sells more than a few products online, you will also have to work with database administrators.

If you want to sell an automated service online, you will find yourself working with software architects and software developers.

From there you will learn about shared and dedicated hosting and about the plethora of services (and pricing) available to you as a hosting customer.

The key in these communications is that each of these professionals owes you, as their customer a clear explanation of the business value which they are providing for the money which you are paying them.

This may be an unfamiliar concept to many techies who grew up in the public school system. Remember, there are always more vendors for a willing customer.

In many ways, IT is the easiest challenge you will face, because so many entrepreneurs have trodden the path before you. An entire industry exists to market IT services to entrepreneurs. You only have to decide what to buy.

Selling Online - Successfully

Once your have negotiated with your suppliers and you have you distribution system arranged -- now comes the difficult part. Now you must bridge the gap between your business and your customers.

Most Internet traffic is currently brokered by search engines, such as Google, Yahoo, and MSN. To do well in business on the Internet, you must do well in the search engines.

This means appearing very early in the search results for the key words or phrases your potential customers will use to shop for your good or services.

Very few potential customers will look for you by name. You must determine the phrases which potential customers will type into the search engines and make sure that you rank well in the result listings for those phrases.

Product types or names are common search phrases, such as "sleeping bags" or "bumper stickers." Key phrases for services often include a geographic component, such as "real estate kansas city" or "house painter colorado springs."

Once your key phrases are defined, you must make certain that your company's web presence is optimized for those phrases. This consist of two sets of tasks: on-site optimization and off-site optimization.

On-site optimization is designing your web site to be focused on those key phrases. This is where your web site designer will work with a professional in the field of Search Engine Optimization (SEO).

Off-site optimization consists of networking with others in your field to make sure they know about your web site -- and that they link to your web site.

The top search engines use the number of links to a web site as one of the criteria for determining which web sites to rank highly in the search results. A SEO specialist can help you in this task, but no one will know your industry as well as you.

Search Engine Optimization (SEO) is critical to the success of an online business. The difference between ranking third and thirtieth for your key phrase is significant revenue for your business.

The eBay Alternative

The tasks involved in setting up a web site and driving traffic towards it can be time consuming and resource intensive for a small business. The time delay imposed by website development and search engine marketing can require many months to begin to deliver ROI.

Many web entrepreneurs use eBay and other online auction houses to short-cut this process and begin selling to online customers almost immediately.

On eBay, you create auctions for the products you are selling and potential buyers bid to determine what they will pay. You are able to set minimum prices to ensure that you will not sell products at prices below your necessary profit margin. You are also able to set up dutch auctions where you are able to sell large quantities of the same item.

The options involved in becoming a successful entrepreneur on the web are extensive. Picking the right path for you own journey is your first step on the road to online success.

Stock Trade Opportunities

In my earlier book on stocks, "A Simple Guide To Investing in Turnaround Stocks: How to Successfully Invest in Stocks of Turnaround Companies" I mentioned that diversification-investing in stocks can be part of a diversified portfolio.

An entrepreneur should be interested in stock investment especially turnaround stocks or stock options as mentioned in my second book, "Options Trading Basics Explained: Understanding the Concepts of Options".

The investment funds can be divided among several solid stocks such as blue chip stocks and the like. By keeping a diversified portfolio, the investor minimizes the risks.

CHAPTER 9

How to Become a Successful Entrepreneur and Avoid the Mistakes of Others

"Do not focus on numbers. Focus on doing what you do best. It's about building a community who want to visit your site every day because you create value and offer expertise." - Cassey Ho

Home based business opportunities are everywhere. Between MSN, Yahoo, and Google alone, over 1,100 people search for the key phrase "home based business" every day. There are a lot of home based business opportunities out there such as affiliate marketing, multi-level marketing, network marketing, pyramid schemes, and many others. I would like to offer you tips to finding the right one for you.

First, you need to find out just how much time you have to work your home based business opportunity. Some opportunities can take more time than they actually say.

The best thing to do would be to contact the owner of the site and find out exactly how much time is necessary to become successful in the business. Many marketers will tell you that they only spend an hour a day promoting their product, as that may be possible it is not likely.

To be successful in anything in life you must work at it. Realistically an online marketer should expect to spend close to 3-4 hours a day to be able to promote their business successfully. The more you work/promote the more you will make.

Second, you should find out exactly what you will be doing once you have started your business. Many companies will hide their opportunity behind smoke and mirrors until you pay for your business, then later you find out you have entered into something you do not want to be a part of.

Check it out. Get the full scoop on the opportunity. Contact the owner and find out what it entails. Ask as many questions as it takes for you to feel confident about your future with the company.

Thirdly, you should be able to trust your "mentor" or your "up-line", talk to them, make sure they are a trust worthy person. Ask them questions about the opportunity and find out what they are like.

There are few mentors on the internet that are actually able to help their students. Send them an e-mail and see how long it takes them to respond Make sure they are the one that can help you and be there when you need them.

Last of all, take some time, sit back and make sure you are doing the right thing before you jump into something you may regret. As mentioned above, ask questions and share your concerns. If you don't like what you are hearing then turn around and go the other way. Your time is to precious to waste with something that doesn't work for you.

Make sure you choose the right home based business opportunity for you. Many people will turn to the internet to fix all their problems and make their dreams come true.

Making money online can be quick, easy, and very accessible to anyone, just don't jump into one uneducated or you may end up paying for it. There are a lot of home based businesses out there, so don't be scared to ask questions. Feel free to ask me any questions you may have as well.

CHAPTER 10

Sourcing for Money to Start Your Business

"When in doubt, bootstrap. Using your own personal resources is the easiest way to start a business. You don't have to convince investors about the merits of your idea. You just have to convince yourself." - Ryan Holmes

When it comes to obtaining financial capital to help your company grow, today's small business owners are stuck between a rock and a hard place. Our economy is stuck in a credit crunch.

Loan growth continues to decelerate. Banks are overly suspicious of borrowers due to the crisis they've experienced in the housing industry.

People that are qualified to receive a bank loan may not be approved due to lack of a strong relationship with the bank, or may be approved for a lot less than they've requested. If your business is just getting started, you're probably in need of some extra funds to help you get growing.

If you haven't attempted to secure a business loan yet, you're in for a rude awakening when you do. Bottom line: financial capital is HARD to come by these days.

As a result, a lot of potentially successful business ideas by aspiring entrepreneurs are either cancelled, put to hold or worst, never made possible not because they did not want to but because they never had a chance to secure funds to start their business.

There are various ways for you to secure the necessary capital that your business you just have to think out of the box, prepare and do a lot of research if you are really determined to turn your business idea into reality.

While there are many sources of money for a small business, some are more accessible than others. Below is a list of 10 common sources of money:

1. Personal Savings
2. Release Equity in Your Home
3. Government Initiatives
4. Buying on Credit

5. Leasing
6. Friends, Relatives and Business Associates
7. Banks
8. Other Commercial Lenders
9. Venture Capitalists
10. The Seller of an Existing Business

When you think you are ready to start your business, the key is to 'keep an eye on your pennies'. What that means is before you get all hyped and spend huge sum of your hard earned money, understand that you will need time to learn if your business is viable or not as it can be a mistake to pour in too much money at the beginning.

It is a fact that a number of small businesses have failed, because they raised and spent a pile of money for an untested business. This could be an entrepreneur's nightmare especially if you are hooked up on borrowed funds. While engaging in business involves risks, there are ways you can minimize these risks by being wise.

Even though some businesses require a great deal of cash, there are still a lot of ventures that do not. It would be better to consider about starting your business small and cheaply as possible.

Think of it this way, that if your concept works, more funds will be available for you and if not, you can move on and take advantage of the lessons you've learned and you won't be burdened with a ton of debts.

Also, a good way to plan for your business is to make an accurate business plan; a well-made business plan will be your prediction tool and will project your business from start up to even 3 to 5 years from now.

A professionally made plan with clearly projected income and cash flow statements with the needed financial data's such as furniture, fixtures, eQuipments, utilities, salary expenses, legal and professional fees, licenses and permits, taxes, rents, advertising, maintenance and repairs, accounting and all other expenses included could help convince and persuade investors, lenders, or any interested people that you have taken into consideration every detail of the costs of the business.

Overall, the plan gives you a sense of security that you have the plan in your hands, you just have to execute the plan to make the business possible

When you already you have your plan, you now have to understand the various factors or keys for you to be able to acquire and secure funds not only to start but also the growth of your business.

To make sure that you will be able to turn your business idea into reality, here are the 7 keys to Funding Your Own Business:

Character - Are you worth the investment? Do you give the impression you will make your plans a reality?. You have to make sure that you took everything into consideration, you have everything planned out and you will be reliable enough.

Ability - You may have the plan but not the money. But another factor that investors will look at is if you and your people have the right skills to make this plan possible. Are you experienced enough or do you have the potential to do what is stated in the plan?

Means - What are the business's assets what and your own personal assets? You must particularly specify what assets are owned by the business as they can be used as collateral for your loans.

Purpose - You then have to specify what is the purpose of the loan? Is it for a sensible cash-generating plan? Few lenders will lend money to pay debts or to give yourself a nice pay rise.

Amount - How much will you need? Your business plan will show you a projected amount so that you will be able to identify the right amount of money needed. What funds will you put in to reduce the lender's risk?

Explain the business carefully, it is important to explain the risks, the threats and how you will be able to manage and reduce the risks for the business.

Repayment - Prove you will be able to repay the money with a realistic cash flow forecast. Such as how much you will pay, either monthly, by quarter, semi-annually or annually. Identifying and calculating the costs or different payment methods will help you choose the right repayment method and also ensure great income for you & the business.

Insurance - Investors and lenders are wary of under-insured businesses. An uninsured loss could destroy you, your credibility and your ability to avail of future loans after all.

Understanding these factors and taking them well into consideration by preparing will give you a better chance at being able to secure funds not only for the start but for the future of your business.

There are various ways to secure funds but always remember that it is advisable to start small from your personal savings, prove the model and then seek JV partnerships for growth and expansion. In business, an entrepreneur takes risks but a successful entrepreneur invests and risks wisely.

Let's first look at the most common form of bank loan for small businesses: a line of credit loan. LoC loans are flexible, negotiable, and quite useful for things like restocking inventory or paying a vendor's bill before receiving a customer's payment. A line of credit works by acquiring an upper limit borrowing amount from your bank.

This amount is based on your credit score and your ability to repay that loan (your income potential). You can borrow against this upper limit while making payments towards reconciling your outstanding balance. For example, you could secure a $25,000 line of credit for your business.

You don't actually receive a lump sum of $20,000. Instead, the LoC allows you to access funds up to $20,000 over time. It helps to understand this type of loan by comparing it to obtaining and making payments on your credit card.

These types of loans are extremely useful for new businesses who may be struggling to obtain a "lump sum" type of loan, so it's definitely worth checking out.

What do you do if you need a lump sum of cash right now and have unsuccessfully attempted to obtain a business loan? Generally speaking, even if you have excellent credit and run a historically successful business, banks don't like approving loans under $25,000; it's not worth their time.

If you need $15,000 right now, you need to look into a business cash advance. A business can choose this option if it currently accepts credit card payments through their merchant account provider.

The account provider will leverage the business's credit card processing history against the amount of funding requested, and the cash advance is given based on processing strength.

The higher your processing receipts are, the more you'll qualify for. Your account provider gets reimbursed by collecting portions of your credit card processing receipts each month. Most business cash advances are collateral-free and are much easier to secure than a bank loan.

The typical turnaround time between submitting an application and receiving your funds is generally around 72 hours.

If it comes down to it, you may even consider using your own credit card to finance certain business purchases. This is the least desirable option considering the usually small line of credit available, not to mention most credit cards have astronomically high interest rates. However, if all else fails and you need to make important payments immediately, it is an option to consider.

How about exploring the possibility of getting a grant? The truth about securing grant funding for starting a business is much simpler, and the programs are less common, than these scammers would have you believe.

First of all, there are some grant opportunities available for starting some businesses, though most often not in the form of direct cash grants. Grant funding generally comes through two sources - private foundations or the government.

Private foundations usually focus on a fairly narrow set of issues, and those issues are generally handled by other nonprofit organizations. Thus, the bulk of their grant funding is earmarked to assist existing nonprofits in furthering their stated purpose.

Government grants can spring from all levels of government - federal, state, and even local. Hundreds of different government branches offer thousands of different grant programs, but very, very few are earmarked for launching a for-profit business.

The majority of federal money that is set aside to help entrepreneurs is not available to individuals. Rather, that funding goes to regional and local nonprofits that provide various programs for first-time entrepreneurs.

The largest chunk of government cash available for entrepreneurs goes to the SBA, where it is redistributed through the various SBA loan programs. Startup funding through the SBA is an excellent option if your idea is well-developed and your personal credit history is good.

Basically, approval by the SBA makes it easier to secure a bank loan for startup...they guarantee the loan (usually a portion of the total amount) so that the bank's risk is reduced. The SBA does have one direct grant program, but it is reserved for established businesses that meet certain other requirements.

The other nonprofits who receive federal funds to help entrepreneurs are charged with the responsibility of making the most difference with the limited funds they are provided. Thus, the grant funding is often used to offer classes in starting a small business, to provide resources for entrepreneurs, or for micro-loan programs, but very rarely offer direct grants to small business startups.

As a rule, you cannot depend on grant funds to finance your startup. Of course, like all rules there are a few exceptions. Many struggling communities have economic development organizations that do provide startup funding in the form of forgivable loans.

That is, as long as your startup meets certain criteria, usually related to providing a certain number of full-time employment positions within a certain amount of time, you may not have to pay back all or any of the original loan.

The federal government also has a few direct grant programs aimed at startup companies doing business in certain foreign countries.

Again, there are generally limitations on what you can do with the money and very specific requirements for the type and operations of the startups that qualify for this money.

There are also a few federal direct grant programs for very specific fields. Some money is available for specific hi-tech research and development, particularly related to governmental needs (defense, healthcare, etc.).

Information on many federal grant programs is available at www.Grants.gov. The site is easy to navigate by key word or just to browse.

You will note that the majority of grant programs are available only to nonprofit organizations, not to individual entrepreneurs.

The bottom line is that the vast majority of new businesses cannot and will not be funded through grants. There is no such thing as "free money" - even the few direct grant programs available come with significant requirements and strings attached. Do not spend one red cent on the "grant finder" scams.

Any money that is available in your community or field can be found through basic research and networking on your own. Anyway, the money you would drop on the grant scams is probably a good start on financing your startup!

CHAPTER 11

Does Branding Your Business Matters?

"It's important to realize that brand is much more than a logo and slogan. A brand is who your company is: how you function and make decisions." - Joanna McFarland

If the question "Branding - should I or shouldn't I?" has ever come up in your mind, I would like to take a few minutes and explain to you what branding is.

Branding is not for everyone, but it is for the business owner who wants to rise up above his competitors. It is the difference between obscurity and recognition.

Your brand is an image that makes its way into your customers' heads that influence how they think and buy. It is based on the promise people believe about you, and the reputation they link with your name and products as the result of all the times and ways they have come into contact with you, your name, your logo or any aspect of your brand.

Branding is the use of advertising, distinctive design or mark, and other means to make consumers easily identify your business upon seeing your design or mark. It also involves promotion to make customers associate your products or services with your business.

In the face of competition it is important to make your business stand out, to set it apart from the competitors. That is the only way to survive and remain competitive in the market.

Who are you? What makes you different from everyone else that does what you do? Why buy from you versus your competitor? And when I see that color scheme, hear that voice or that song, see that logo or visit that page, do I immediately think of you and your business? Do I feel good about it?

Branding your business should be a goal from the time you conceive of starting your online business. You don't need a final product or a service before you start thinking through this process of creating your online branding strategy.

Countless new Internet marketers start their businesses with products in mind, markets in mind or customers in mind.

All of these are good solid things to consider, but they leave out the most important part of the equation.

The name of the game now is how people, especially your target market, associate your business, product or service as a symbol of quality, dependability and fast but efficient service, coupled with total customer satisfaction.

A firm that does not brand its business, product or service will just decay and die.

To brand your business is to promote or advertise it, or by having a distinctive design or logo, for the purpose of creating awareness and recognition of your customers.

This can be done by:

a. Creating an image or logo, with color combination: This includes your logo, your stationary, and even your building style. You should have a certain image for your business that accurately reflects your company as it is.

If you are an elegant style locale, then you will want to make sure that every piece of correspondence reflects that elegance, and you will want to make sure your business building is in keeping with the same style.

Whatever image you choose to represent, be consistent in all things. If you always display the same image, people will begin to equate that image with you and your business. This will create the type of branding that you want for your company.

b. Making a tagline or motto

c. Marketing, advertising and promotion

For example, if you mention a fast food restaurant, what brand would first come into your mind? If you need a tooth paste, what brand do you buy? Or if you want to rent-a-car, what car rental company will you call?

In the face of competition it is important to make your business stand out, to set it apart from the competitors. That is the only way to survive and remain competitive in the market.

The name of the game now is how people, especially your target market, associate your business, product or service as a symbol of quality, dependability and fast but efficient service, coupled with total customer satisfaction.

A Brand is a promise that you make to the consumer. There are three very important things that you need to remember when entering the branding arena.

- Your brand is created when you build trust in the unique promise about who you are, what you stand for and what distinctive, significant benefits you deliver.
- Your brand is built by living up to this promise each and every time your customer comes into contact with your name, your message or your business.
- Your brand is strengthened when you constantly reinforce your brand promise.

Brands create relationships between the customer and the product which withstand price wars, rise above offers from new competitors and in some rare cases forgive the slip in product or service excellence.

A firm that does not brand its business, product or service will just decay and die.

If you walk into an Apple store, no one needs to sell you ANYTHING. You are simply choosing what you want to buy. You can't put a price on that!

So as you develop your online business, from the start, continue to ask yourself the questions; Is this consistent with the image I am trying to create, with the message I am trying to convey, with the reputation i am trying to build. Does it support my overall vision and mission statement?

It should be quite obvious how important it is to develop an effective online branding strategy early on in your business. Now you need to figure out how.

You can brand yourself on the go or later on, but you will be swimming up stream. Why not make branding your business a priority NOW. Everything else becomes easier if you do.

Branding using promotional products: Promoting your business is one of the primary keys to solvency. There is no point in having a product or service to offer on the marketplace if you don't let anyone know it exists.

It is the responsibility of the promotions department in your business organization to let the public know you have products and to create a demand for those products. Using promotional products is a tactic for branding your organization correctly.

Branding your business is an essential part of promotions since it involves getting the public familiar with your company name or logo and having it invoke a feeling of trust and confidence when it is seen.

Delivering more or better than you promised is the foundation for creating the reaction you want when people see your logo. People that receive promotional items as gifts are eager to show them off because the items are unique.

Once you have established a reputation for excellent service by going the extra step for your customers, they will automatically associate your logo with reliability and dependability. Compound that with giving them a free gift and you gain far more in goodwill than you ever would with an expensive ad campaign.

People certainly appreciate getting things for free, and when you give items away emblazoned with your logo, the return on your investment increases exponentially.

Promotional apparel such as custom t-shirts and hats are the popular promotional products since logo exposure is extremely high. People appreciate the value of the gift and willingly wear the item while displaying your information.

Writing instruments also make great gifts because they are functional items that people will use where others can see your logo. Promotional bags such as tote bags, back packs and computer bags are well-received as gifts in the same way because of their usefulness.

Other popular promotional items include drink ware, desk accessories, calendars, magnets, computer or electronics accessories, sporting goods and automotive accessories.

Promotional products companies can help you determine the best strategy for branding your logo. They will recommend the best items for your particular industry and will consider the demographics for the group that will receive the items.

They can supply just about any item you need where your logo can be imprinted and they can do all of this within your marketing budget.

Familiarity with your brand leads to a loyal customer base especially when you can be trusted to deliver top notch products and services. Your customers will not hesitate to spread the good news about your company and in this way become part of your greatest sales force.

However, you like so many other new business owners are probably unsure of how or what action items to use when branding your business.

Though there are an endless number of theories available most marketing and branding professionals agree that the ten most crucial building blocks of branding your business are as follows:

1. Discover your values
2. Recognise your mission
3. Identify your ideal client
4. Build an emotional and personal connection
5. Work to clarify the benefits you offer vs. the features you include
6. Provide an experience for your clients or customer
7. Send a message; support a belief
8. Be consistent
9. Think creatively and have the strength to reinvent yourself and your brand
10. Avoid trends, consumers are critical and imitation can result in doubt

CHAPTER 12

Legal Aspect of Your Business

This is one area of business where the saying "Anything worth doing well - is worth doing right" is so true. Filing your business name paperwork correctly is critical to obtaining business credit. If you do it wrong, you could give someone else the ability to use your business name or even take it from you once you have your company established.

In setting up a business, one of the most important decisions you have to make is to choose the type of business structure you will have such as Sole Proprietorship, Partnership, Limited Liability Company or Corporation. The type of business structure is an important determinant on how your business will operate and for taxation purposes.

If you decided on a Sole Proprietorship or Partnership structure type of business, you have to register it by filing a form called DBA (Doing Business As) or FBN (Fictitious Business Name). This is dependent on the state where the business is being formed where you have to apply for the necessary licenses and permits as may be required.

If your business is a corporation or Limited Liability Company, you have to register it with the Secretary of State as such and a corresponding number will be given when the formation documents are filed. This number is most likely called the Secretary of State File Number.

If you have employees, you also need to get a number from your state's Employment Development Department to allow you to deal with payroll issues.

If you own and operate a business, you may be required to obtain a Federal Employer Identification Number (EIN) and should consider doing so even if not required. Commonly referred to as a federal tax ID number, an EIN is like a social security number for your business.

Just as your social security number is used to identify you as a unique individual by government, financial and other institutions, an employer identification number is used to identify a business as a unique entity by government, financial, tax and regulatory agencies.

Obtaining and using an EIN to identify your business to the Internal Revenue Service and the various federal agencies that regulate businesses is a smart way to separate and differentiate between your personal and business obligations and liabilities.

Issued by the IRS as a tax identification number, an EIN is a unique identifier assigned and tied to the individual owner of a specific business. EINs are used by employers, sole proprietors, corporations, partnerships, non-profits, government agencies and certain other business entities.

By using an EIN to identify their business, sole proprietors who have been using their social security number as both a personal and business identifier can create an important layer of legal separation and privacy between their personal and business affairs.

Using an EIN rather than a social security number for business transactions prevents access to the personal information tied to your social security number.

An EIN provides the additional benefit of creating a continuous business identity even if the name, focus or location of your business changes. This allows business owners to capitalize on tax, financial or regulatory advantages developed in previous years.

As long as business ownership and operating status do not change, your EIN follows your business through the inevitable cosmetic and directional changes that accompany the definition and growth of a business. You can use the same EIN even if you change the name or address of your business or add additional locations.

However, because an EIN is issued to the specific owner of a business and not to the business itself, a change in ownership necessitates obtaining a new EIN. A new EIN must also be obtained if the status of your business changes; for instance, if you incorporate your business or take on partners and begin operating as a partnership. A new EIN is also required when a business files for bankruptcy or establishes a profit sharing or retirement plan.

Despite its name, you do not need to be an employer to obtain an employer identification number. You are required to obtain an EIN if your business operates as a corporation or partnership or you offer taxable products or services, collect sales tax, have employees, withhold taxes on income, have a Keogh plan or file any type of federal tax return.

However a business owner can apply for an EIN even if not required and will generally find it to his advantage. An EIN is required on income tax forms, employment tax reports, social security records and tax payments and is required to apply for a business license. Most banks also require an EIN to open a business account.

The application procedure is simple and painless. While you can apply for an EIN by contacting your local IRS office and filling out form SS-4, online application is fast and easy. Available at http://www.irs.gov, the EIN application form can be completed online.

As soon as you complete the online application, you will receive your EIN and can begin using it immediately. Make certain you download, save and print the EIN confirmation page.

Because it takes about two weeks from the date of issuance for a new EIN to be fully integrated into the IRS data base, business owners must wait two to three weeks before filing electronic returns or making electronic payments.

The EIN is a federal identification number. While many states also use the federal EIN, some require state identification numbers.

An Employer ID Number (EIN), also known as a federal tax identification number is used as an identification number for other purposes, including filing state tax returns. This is an IRS requirement in order to operate.

Applying for an EIN for your business is very easy by filling in IRS Form SS-4. You can apply for an EIN online, by telephone, by fax, or by mail. If you submit your application online, you will receive your EIN at the same time and use it immediately.

Information regarding the types of business licenses you need to operate may be obtained from the state, city, county, or town wherein you plan to conduct business. The license requirements depend on the types of businesses you want to operate.

For a comprehensive list of these requirements, you can visit the United States Small Business Administration (SBA) website at http://www.sba.gov, which will provide you a list of where to obtain necessary information about business licenses for your state. Additional information is also available from your city and county's web sites.

There is paperwork involved in this process, and it needs to be done right. This is one of those times when you want to make sure everything is double checked for accuracy.

First, make sure you have what you need to set up your business. Here's a quick checklist to make sure you look like a real business and not a "hobby".

Company Name - Your business must have a name that is available for use in your State. You cannot register your business entity if someone else has already used the name you choose.

You can find out if your name is available by going onto your State's website and doing an entity name search.

For example, in Michigan you would go onto their website michigan.gov. If your name is available, then you make the decision at this point what business structure is going to be best for your business (i.e. corporation, LLC, etc.). Generally, you can obtain the forms you need to register by going onto your State's website and down-loading them for free.

Address - Your business needs a real address, not a P.O. box or UPS address. You can use your home address if you wish, but the main idea is that your address needs to be a physical address that can accept mail for your company. The address you register with the State must be the same address you use when you apply for business lines of credit or vendor credit (like a Home Depot card).

Tax Payer ID Number - After you have registered your company with the State in which you are going to do business, you must then get your Employer ID number (EIN) from the Internal Revenue Service.

This EIN is the number that you will use when you apply for business credit. You will not use your social security number (unless you are a sole proprietor) on business applications.

Phone Number - Once you have registered with the State, and obtained your EIN from the IRS, you should get a separate phone number dedicated to your business. This phone number must be listed in the national "411" directories with the same name and address that you registered with the State.

When you call to set up your new phone line, be sure your use your EIN and not your social security number. You should not use your cell phone number as your primary business number.

Lending institutions will generally call "411" to verify that the name and phone number you list on your application matches the information that they find on the State website where your business is registered. If there are discrepancies in the information provided, you may not be able to obtain any business credit.

Remember, there are possible tax implications that could hurt you or your business if you set up your company incorrectly.

A tax professional may be able to answer your specific questions on the advantages and disadvantages of each of the business structures that are available and can help you decide which one is the best for you financially.

If you need to get an Employer Identification Number for your business you can apply in any of the following ways:

Apply Online - Companies can apply for their EIN number by using the EIN online service. Customers simply need to go to the EIN online website and fill out all the required fields on the application form, perform a simple and preliminary validation and then submit the correct SS4 form.

Once the IRS has checked it for all the correct information an EIN will be issued. Note however that not all business entities can apply online so read through the website before applying.

Apply by Mail - If you prefer to do things the old fashioned way then you can still send in your EIN application by mail. The turnaround on an EIN application by mail is about four weeks and again, you need to make sure that the SS4 has been filled out very carefully with all the required information.

If it is decided that your business needs an EIN it will be mailed back with the number included.

Apply by Fax - You can also fax your completed SS4 form to your IRS state fax number once you have ensured it is correctly filled out. If everything is OK with the SS4 and it is decided to allocate you an EIN then it will be faxed back to you within four business days.

Apply by Phone - Lastly, you can also apply for your EIN by phone. This is the route most taxpayers choose as it is very quick. You simply call a toll-free number (800-829-4933) between 7:00am and 5:00pm local time and an operator will take down your details and if everything is in order, will give you the number there and then over the phone.

CHAPTER 13

Marketing Your Business as an Entrepreneur

"Selling is not a pushy, winner-takes-all, macho act. It is an empathy-led, process-driven, and knowledge-intensive discipline. Because, in the end, people buy from people." - Subroto Bagchi

Marketing can be compared to motor oil in a car. If it is applied correctly it keeps your sales machine working at peak efficiency. Most sales people however tend to confuse marketing with branding or think the two are one and the same. This belief could not be farther from the truth.

Wikipedia defines marketing as "the process used to determine what products or service may be of interest to customers, and the strategy to use in sales, communication, and business development."

The key to having a diverse, multichannel marketing strategy is to concentrate on your brand. It is the one aspect that you can control amidst the ever-changing internet. Google will keep on launching updates, Facebook may change how posts get impressions, YouTube may alter its search algorithm, and so on.

You won't be able to control these changes, but you can have full control of your brand.

Attracting and growing a loyal audience should be your main concern if you wish to take the reins. By exposing your brand to as many online mediums, your business is guaranteed to stay relevant.

In addition to exposing your brand via social media, you can create your own website, use organic SEO strategies, and market your brand though press releases, blog articles, banner ads, pay-per-click ads, video streaming sites, and emails.

You should consider every single one of these strategies as a backup plan, just in case one of them compromises your goal of building an audience.

If any of these individual channels stop delivering the expected results, you can minimize its effects and cover up any losses in traffic with other channels.

A multichannel marketing strategy will surely pay off. Initially, it will cost you time and money. But if it means that your brand will eventually be recognized across several online mediums with little effort, it is worth your while.

Using various channels to market your brand also gives your business the ability to persist regardless of the changes they might force yourself into.

Marketing your brand-new business is essential but it can be difficult to get your company's name out there. Here are some easy steps to get you started.

1. Think about your customer. Who is he or she (or it if your company serves other companies)? What does your customer need that your company fulfill? Put yourself in the customer's shoes: Where would you go to look for the services your company provides?
2. Explore marketing options: Phone book ads, flyers, newspaper advertisements, radio or television spots, internet advertising, postcards, trade shows etc. The possibilities are truly endless.

   Consider how often each of these options will appear before your potential customers. Consider how many potential customers will see your item. Be sure to also consider the cost for each item and whether you can reuse the item later on.

3. Now that you have a good idea of how much each item will cost, create a marketing/advertising budget. If you have a new business, your budget may be quite small, but you may find many inexpensive opportunities to help get you started.

4. Also be sure to consider your competition. Where do they advertise? Is there anything they do that you can improve upon? If another company has a cheesy-looking ad, you can position your company as the high-quality alternative. If the competition has an elite-look, position your company as the lower-cost alternative.

5. Once you have a good idea of marketing costs, consider whether you want to go it alone or hire a professional.

   If you have a marketing/advertising/public relations background you may well be able to do it yourself. However, you should consider hiring a professional if you don't have the time or experience to create your product or if you still don't have a clear idea of what you want to do.

6. Consider the many free, or almost free, ways to introduce your company: Tell friends, family members and colleagues. Networking is the best way to spread the word: It's free and if people like you, they will probably like your company.

   You can also try article marketing on the internet (write articles for free article content websites that include a link to your company's website), posting fliers, or even using a "30-second sound bite" about your company in elevator or cocktail party conversations.

   Another free avenue is to take part in local civic groups, such as chambers of commerce or downtown development authorities. These groups exist to promote local businesses.

7. For business-to-business companies, consider cold calling. While many people hate the practice, there's nothing like it for those who persevere.

Write a brief script about your company and its services and then use it when calling companies. It may take hundreds of calls but in the meantime you may be planting seeds that will blossom into future success.

The important things to remember with these tips are patience and planning. You will need to plan your marketing budget and stick with it, especially at first. Recognize that it will take time for your business to grow, so plan accordingly.

However, these steps will help you get the word out about your new venture.

Do you know when starting a new website, one of the most important decisions you've got to make is choosing the right domain name to market or promote your brand online, as it will impact your business's success in virtually every possible way. Having a powerful domain is so important for better business growth, long term establishment, sales and credibility.

Getting the right domain has to become the first priority for any business that has to achieve overall recognition. From search engine optimization and social media marketing your domain name is one great marketing tool that can help your brand do a lot more on the web.

You would not want to confuse your online visitors because your domain id seems to be completely different from your site's name, especially when you are setting up an e-commerce website as at times business owners are quite neglectful when considering the domain name for an online store.

Please note that the consequences of selecting an inappropriate domain name can be just as disturbing as having no contact us page on your website.

When choosing a domain name, there are certain factors that must be considered in order to ensure an effective domain name that supports your brand and online marketing strategy.

Search engines and directories are the most powerful online marketing communication mode, so before you register the domain consider how your domain name choice affects site placement.

The majority of directories simply list the links to home pages in an alphabetical order. You can also consider selecting a domain name with a letter of the alphabet that's near to the beginning like "a", "b" or "c" for instance "axact.com" will come way before "rightsolutions.com ".

Nevertheless, check the directories before you choose a domain name. You may find the directories already cluttered with such domain names that are starting with the letter "a".

You must also know that search engines do scan websites and sort the results based on key words.

When beginning a new business, one may even want to go for a good domain first. As the likelihood to first choose a business name and then expect the domain to be available.

Keyword domains have been the first choice for SEO's and search engine marketers who've been purchasing such domains for the reason of better CTR's which can help to achieve improved rankings on Google, Bing and Yahoo.

Whether you're a marketer who wants to build a brand or an individual who wants to run a blog / forum or e-commerce website the very presence of a keyword phrase in a domain name is itself one big ranking factor. But sadly, Google has taken strict notice of this practice which is why EMD's aren't as popular as they used to be.

Although there is certainly a branding advantage of including a relevant keyword in your domain name, Moreover, in some cases having a good keyword domain can increase one's chances of Click-Through Rates (CTR's) and SERP listings.

The guidelines below will help you understand the intricacies involved in selecting the right domain name for your website when developing your brand.

First and foremost- Make it brief: A domain name that's small will be easy to remember as customers viewing your site in a matter of seconds can grasp more information from it. Having long names can look good to an extent but are definitely hard to remember.

For instance Google Webs or Wix are small and unforgettable names for a domain and are known for their successful online business.

Should have a positive image: The name you've selected for your domain should be lively and must deliver positive vibes.

Your domain name is your building doorway and should be appealing, representing your desired image. And if that's not the case your brand name or the domain name needs to be changed.

Should be unique and authoritative: Avoid using names similar to the names being used by other companies; as such names can cause legal problems. At the very least, consumers may get confused and patronize your competition.

Words have implicit meanings and connotations, prior to finalizing a domain name a little research can help to ensure that your domain name perfectly communicates your desired message.

So, the domain name that completely reflects the brand image and the information in an authoritative manner will be the right way to select a brand name as consistency in brands, products and domain ID's help a lot in making a brand memorable!

Moreover, your domain name must be easy to spell as users are able to easily recollect your brand/domain name.

There is need to avoid the use of the following when setting up your domain ID:

Numbers should be avoided (either written TWO or the numeric 2)

Confusing and difficult words to spell

Avoid the use of hyphens

The process of choosing a suitable domain name can be quite difficult and time consuming. Organizations with heftier marketing budgets can afford shorter and more appropriate domain names, and can also spend more on SEO and content.

The guidelines listed above can set the parameters in selecting the right domain name to market your brand. However, in the majority of cases the best names for a domain which have a strong brand appeal are already registered and have an absolutely exorbitant price when you look at their price tag.

Brainstorming sessions generate many great ideas and can possibly give you an inkling that on what lines you should be working on. It can be like creating new words or merging two (or more) words that you feel can represent your brand in a better way.

Affect the speed of consumer awareness about your brand, it can influence your market image or play an important role in establishing brand-equity information, and all that's associated to your brand, but it must distinguish you from your competitors and should be able to describe your brand attributes and characteristics.

And to do that you've got to specify your marketing objectives and brand promotion strategy.

CONCLUSION

"You have to see failure as the beginning and the middle, but never entertain it as an end." - Jessica Herrin

Everything in life has two sides like the proverbial two sides of a coin. Entrepreneurship is fraught with dangers, perils, hazards and threats or risks just as it has booties, returns, compensations or incentives also known as rewards.

Here are risks and rewards of entrepreneurship which I would like discuss briefly in this article for the benefit and information of those wishing to embark on the great journey of entrepreneurship:

Risks of Entrepreneurship

Getting Paid - The income of the business enterprise would determine whether the entrepreneur gets paid or not. The entrepreneur does not have the luxury of an assured paycheck like his counterparts in paid employment. If the business does not make profit, there is nothing for the entrepreneur.

Sporadic Income - The start-up entrepreneur may not have enough business to provide him or her with steady income. His or her income may fluctuate from day to day or from month to month.

No Income - An entrepreneur may face a season in his or her business life when there would be no business at all or when customers have failed to meet their payment obligations and therefore no income. Start-up entrepreneurs are usually advised to save at least enough to cover six months expenses and income needs as part of their financial planning.

Having Security - Whatever an entrepreneur has comes from the business. Unlike people in paid employment who may have a compulsory retirement savings account backed by their employer, the entrepreneur has to provide his or her own insurance and retirement security. Before moving from paid employment to full time entrepreneurship, it is important that aspiring entrepreneurs add as part of their financial planning, some element of insurance and retirement security through savings.

Rewards of Entrepreneurship

Passion - Passion they say sells. One of the greatest joys of entrepreneurship is working daily on the passion of your life. When one's work and daily pursuits are in the realm of his or her innate desires, one works with enthusiasm, appetite and hunger that drive to great action.

Apart from being a reward on its own, passion ensures that one is working with boundless energy which leads to greater production.

Great Boss - Entrepreneurs work for the greatest boss on earth which is themselves. In paid employment, we meet all kinds of bosses - some nasty, some great and some boring. The greatest boss anyone would have is oneself. Entrepreneurship enables you work for yourself and that creates an unbeatable feeling which money cannot buy.

Hours - One of the immediate benefits of entrepreneurship is having control of one's life. Though the beginning of entrepreneurship may be rough, the ability to be in charge and have the capacity to set your times and schedules for your work and business is a reward of inestimable value.

The entrepreneur can even keep his location virtual, meaning he may work from the comfort of his own home using the internet. An entrepreneur can also chose to be mobile.

Regardless of the risks associated with entrepreneurship, it is still the way for all those who wish to create wealth and find the greatest possible satisfaction in life pursuits.

I sincerely hope that this book has helped to open your eyes to the wonderful world of entrepreneurship and being your own **BOSS**. I therefore invite you to read my other two publications, "Options Trading Basics Explained: Understanding the Concepts of Options" and "A Simple Guide to Investing in Turnaround Stocks: How to Successfully Invest in Stocks of Turnaround Companies".

From the author's desk: Reviews are gold to authors! If you've enjoyed this Book, would you consider rating it and reviewing it on Amazon.com?

Thanking you in anticipation.

www.ingramcontent.com/pod-product-compliance
Lightning Source LLC
Chambersburg PA
CBHW021829170526
45157CB00007B/2734